Goodbye Preschool, Hello Kindergarten

by

Sonica Ellis

Illustrated by Nejla Shojaie

DEDICATION

This book is dedicated to Maximus Gerikh, and all children starting kindergarten!

Don't be afraid to start something new!

This book belongs to

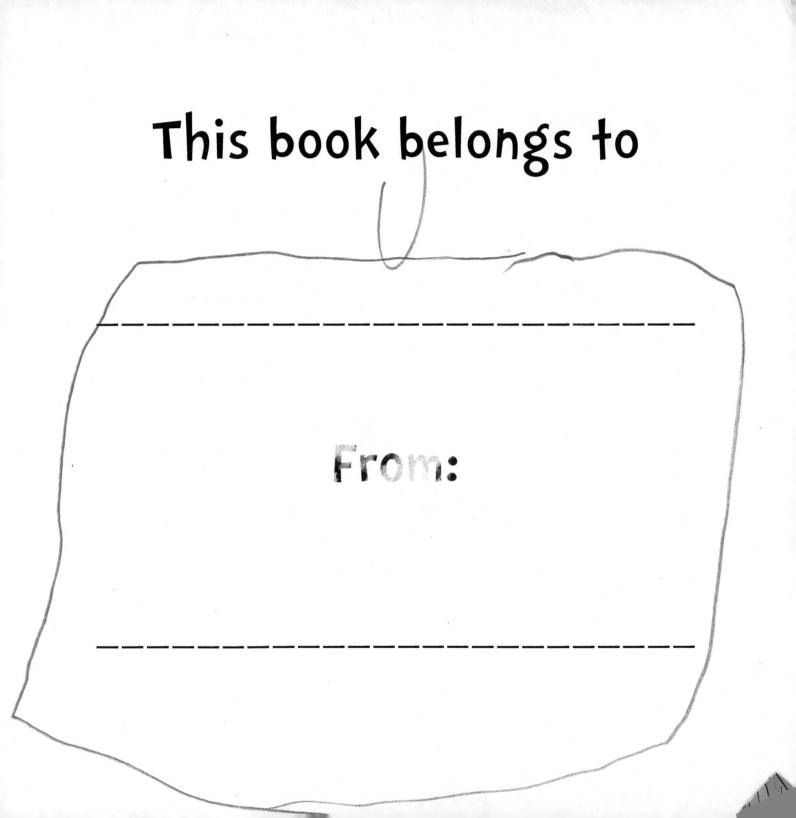

From:

It's time to say "goodbye preschool."
It's time for me to go.

I'm nervous and a little scared
Of all that I don't know.

Change is never easy,
It's hard to say goodbye.
I don't really want to leave,
I'm afraid that I might cry.

I'm going to miss my teachers.
I'm going to miss my friends.
I told my mom and dad I'm sad
And they told me sadness ends.

Kindergarten looks very big,

Much bigger than preschool.

What if I get lost inside
Or forget the Golden Rule?

I do not know this teacher,
Although she does look nice.
She said her name is
Miss Charlene
And then smiled at me twice.

There are lots of girls and boys,
A few I even know.

This may not be that bad at all,
I'll smile and wave "hello."

Miss Charlene finds me a seat
Next to a boy I know.
He looks a little bit unsure
Of just how things will go.

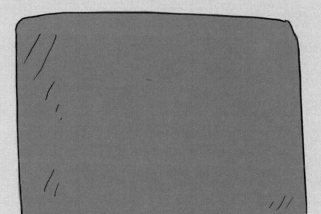

Alphabet Chart

Aa Bb Cc Dd
Ee Ff Gg Hh
Ii Jj Kk Ll
Mm Nn Oo Pp
Qq Rr Ss Tt
Uu Vv Ww
Xx Yy Zz

Aa Bb
Cc

I'm excited now to learn new things,
To try and fail and try again,
To count and sing the alphabet
And draw on paper with a pen.

My old teachers, you are the best.
You showed me so much love.
I never will forget the hugs
Or when you found my missing glove.

I've learned something already here
Of that you can be certain.

Sometimes it's OK not to know
Just what's behind the curtain.

And just because things have to change
It doesn't mean it's bad.
It turns out it is often good,
And knowing this I am glad.

So thank you preschool teachers,
You'll never be forgotten.
I'm in big school now,

Hello

Kindergarten!